What Is a Map?

Monday

1. A drawing of a place from above is a ________.

   bed　　　　　　map

2. The map shows Joey's ________.

   bedroom　　　　　　living room

Tuesday

1. What is on the bed?

2. What is on the toy box?

Wednesday

1. What is next to the rug?

bed

desk

2. What is next to the chair?

window

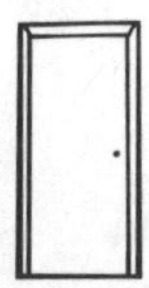
door

What Is a Map?

Thursday

1. What is behind the chair?  

2. What is in front of the chair?  

Friday

1. Where does Joey sleep?

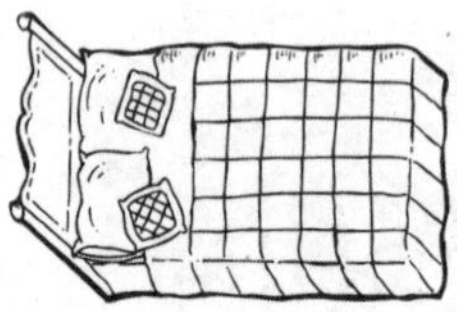
bed

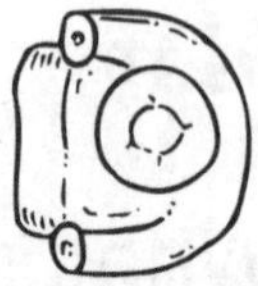
chair

2. Where does Joey color?

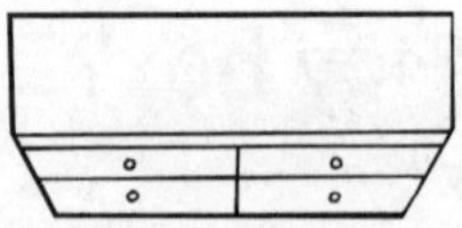
dresser

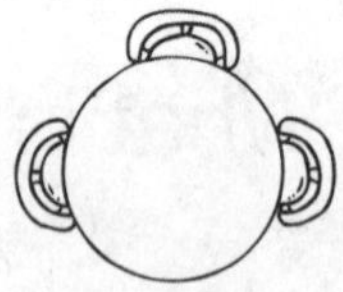
table

Challenge

Color your favorite place in Joey's bedroom.

Using a Map

Monday

1. You use a map to find ________.

   friends places

2. The map shows Mr. Brown's ________.

   bedroom classroom

Tuesday

1. What is in the front of the classroom?

    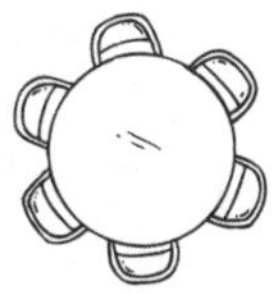

2. What is in the back of the classroom?

    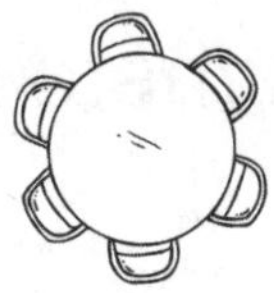

Wednesday

1. What is on the right side of the classroom?

2. What is on the left side of the classroom?

Using a Map

Thursday

1. What is near the reading rug?

   books　　　computers

2. What is far away from the reading rug?

   table　　　teacher's desk

Friday

1. Where does Mr. Brown sit?

   at the sink　　　at the teacher's desk

2. Where does Mr. Brown wash his hands?

   at the computer　　　at the sink

Challenge

Follow directions to color the classroom map.

1. Draw an apple on the teacher's desk.
2. Color the three computers yellow.
3. Mark an X on your favorite student desk.
4. Color blue water in the sink.
5. Draw a pencil on the table.
6. Color the reading rug brown.

Daily Geography

WEEK 3

Finding Places on a Map

Monday

1. The map shows where people ________.

    live   work

2. Apartments are ________.

    cars   homes

Tuesday

1. How many floors are there?

    1   2   3

2. Which apartment is for rent?

    2A   2B   2C

Wednesday

1. What apartment is above the Guzmans?

    2A   2B   2C

2. The Wongs live ________ Mr. and Mrs. Young.

    above   below

Finding Places on a Map

Thursday

1. 1A is on the ________ floor.

   first   second   third

2. The Wongs live on the ________ floor.

   first   second   third

Friday

1. The Johnsons live ________.

   downstairs   upstairs

2. Ms. Carter lives ________.

   downstairs   upstairs

Challenge

1. In which apartment would you like to live? ____________
2. What floor is it on? ______________
3. Color your favorite apartment.

Directions on a Map

Monday

1. The map shows a ________.

   bedroom   school

2. How many directions are on the map?

   1   2   3   4

Tuesday

1. Which direction points up?

   north   south

2. Which direction points down?

   north   south

Wednesday

1. Which direction points right?

   east   west

2. Which direction points left?

   east   west

Directions on a Map

Thursday

1. What is north of the swing set?

   bikes   slide

2. What is east of the tree?

   flag   sandbox

Friday

1. What is west of the sidewalk?

   sandbox   swing set

2. What is south of Franklin School?

   parking lot   playground

Challenge

1. What are the four main directions?

   ______________   ______________

   ______________   ______________

2. Circle the four direction arrows on the map.

Using Directions

Monday

1. The map shows a ________.

   park zoo

2. The compass rose shows ________ directions.

   2 4

Tuesday

1. What letter stands for south?

   N S

2. What letter stands for east?

   E W

Wednesday

1. The letter **W** stands for ________.

   east west

2. The letter **N** stands for ________.

   north south

Daily Geography

WEEK 5

Using Directions

Thursday

1. What is **N** of the cow?

   horse   sheep

2. What is **E** of the cow?

   rabbits   turtles

Friday

1. What is **W** of the sheep? ____________________

2. What is **N** of the turtles? ____________________

Challenge

1. Color the cow black and white.
2. Color the animal north of the cow brown.
3. Color the animals that are east of the cow green.
4. Color the animals that are north and east of the cow yellow.
5. Color the animals that are north and west of the cow tan.
6. Color the animals that are south and east of the cow white.
7. Color the animals that are south and west of the cow pink.

A Map Key

Monday

1. What is the name of the map?

    Pinewood Springs   Rocky Point

2. Which one is on the map key?

hill

Tuesday

1. Which symbol stands for mountain?

2. Which symbol stands for river?

Wednesday

1. Which symbol stands for hill?

2. Which symbol stands for plain?

A Map Key

Thursday

1. What is south of the hills?  

2. What is west of the lake?  

Friday

1. Which one is the highest?

   hill mountain plain

2. Which one is the lowest?

   hill mountain plain

Challenge

The cabin is near trees. They are called woods. Draw a tree on the map key. Write the word **woods** by the tree.

Using a Map Key

Monday

1. What is the name of the map?

   Lake View Park   The Camp

2. How many symbols are on the map key?

   2   4

Tuesday

1. Which symbol stands for lake? 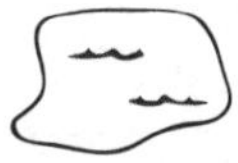 

2. Which symbol stands for camp?  

Wednesday

1. Which symbol stands for woods?  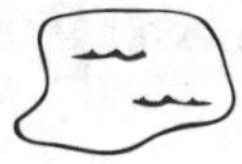

2. What is next to the camp? 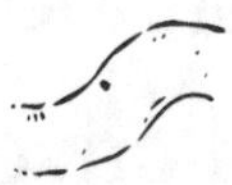 

Using a Map Key

Thursday

1. What is south of the lake?

   camp　　　　　　woods

2. What is east of the camp?

   bear　　　　　　ducks

Friday

1. The woods are ________ of the trail.

   north and east　　　　　　north and west

2. You follow the trail to the ____________________.

Challenge

1. Find the bear in a cave.
2. Draw a cave on the map key.
3. Write the word **cave** by your symbol.

Daily Geography

WEEK 8

Parts of a Map

Monday

1. The title of the map is ________.

   Fire Station   Maria's Neighborhood

2. A map has a title, a compass rose, and a

   ____

Tuesday

1. Which symbol stands for the school?

2. Which symbol stands for Maria's house?

Wednesday

1. Maria lives on ________ Street.

   Low   High

2. What is on Safe Street?

Parts of a Map

Thursday

1. What is east of Maria's house?

2. What is south of the library?

Friday

1. What is on Safe Street and Low Street?

   library   park

2. What runs north and south?

   Low Street   Main Street

Challenge

1. Circle the title of the map.
2. Outline the map key in red.
3. Color the compass rose yellow.

Picturing a Place

Monday

1. The map shows Joey's ________.

    backyard   school

2. Joey's backyard is ________.

    inside   outside

Tuesday

1. Is there a treehouse?   yes   no

2. Is there a table?   yes   no

Wednesday

1. How many swings are there?

    1   2   3

2. What is by the tree?

    sandbox   table

Picturing a Place

Thursday

1. Joey has a ________.

   cat dog

2. What is east of the garden?

   sandbox swing set

Friday

1. What is north of the doghouse?

   table treehouse

2. What is <u>not</u> in Joey's backyard?

   bike sandbox

Challenge

Look at Joey's backyard for one minute. Close your eyes. Think about Joey's backyard. Now open your eyes. Turn the map over so you can't see it. Draw one thing from Joey's backyard.

Daily Geography

WEEK 10

Picturing the United States

Monday

1. The title of the map is ________.

   Our Country — Picturing the United States

2. The map shows ________ of the United States.

   all — part

Tuesday

1. The United States is ________.

   large — small

2. The map shows ________.

   1 state — 50 states

Wednesday

1. Which state is in the north?

   North Dakota — Texas

2. Which state is in the south?

   North Dakota — Texas

Daily Geography

WEEK 10

Picturing the United States

Thursday

1. Virginia is in the ________.

    east　　　　west

2. California is in the ________.

    east　　　　west

Friday

1. Which is larger?

    Alaska　　　　Hawaii

2. The larger states are in the ________.

    east　　　　west

Challenge

What is the name of your state?

____

Color your state on the map.

A Treasure Map

Daily Geography

WEEK 11

Monday

1. What kind of map is it?

   neighborhood map　　treasure map

2. The map shows ________.

   an island　　a sailboat

Tuesday

1. Pete followed a ________.

   route　　street

2. A route is a ________.

   direction　　path

Wednesday

1. Pete started in the ________ part of the island.

   north　　south

2. Pete went through a ________.

cave

hut

A Treasure Map

Thursday

1. What is north of the cave?

2. Pete saw a ________ on his route.

   bear   snake

Friday

1. Where is the treasure?

2. The treasure is on the ________ side of the island.

   north   south

Challenge

1. Trace Pete's route to the treasure.
2. Draw a chest where the treasure is buried.

A Street Map

Monday

1. What is the title of the map?

   Kari's House　　　　A Street Map

2. The map shows a ________.

   neighborhood　　　　state

Tuesday

1. There are ________ houses in the neighborhood.

   2　　　　8

2. Kari and Kim live on ________ Street.

   First　　　　Second

Wednesday

1. The hospital is on ________ Street.

   Second　　　　Third

2. The gas station is on ________ Street.

   Green　　　　Brown

Daily Geography

WEEK 12

A Street Map

Thursday

1. Which street runs north and south?

   Brown Street   First Street

2. Which street runs east and west?

   Green Street   Second Street

Friday

1. The park is not on ________.

   First Street   Third Street

2. Who lives across the street from the park?

   Kim   Kari

Challenge

1. Color Kari's house yellow.
2. Color the school red.
3. Draw Kari's route from home to school in black.

What Is a Globe?

Monday

1. A globe is a model of ________.

   Earth Mars

2. Earth and a globe are both ________.

   round square

Tuesday

1. The Earth has ________.

   only land only water both land and water

2. The globe shows ________.

   only land only water both land and water

Wednesday

1. Large areas of land are ________.

   continents oceans

2. Large bodies of water are ________.

   continents oceans

What Is a Globe?

Thursday

1. Name one continent on the picture of the globe.

   ______________________ America

2. Name one ocean on the picture of the globe.

   ______________________ Ocean

Friday

1. Which ocean is east of North America?

   ____

2. Which ocean is west of South America?

   ____

Challenge

Color the continents green. Color the oceans blue.

A World Map

Monday

1. The map shows ________ of the world.

    all　　　　part

2. The map shows land and ________.

    trees　　　　water

Tuesday

1. There are ________ continents.

    4　　　　7

2. Each continent shows ________.

    an animal　　　　a tree

Wednesday

1. There are ________ oceans.

    5　　　　7

2. A ________ is in the Pacific Ocean.

A World Map

Thursday

1. Which animal is on Africa?

2. Which animal is on South America?

Friday

1. The ________ Ocean is in the north.

   Arctic   Pacific

2. Antarctica is in the ________.

   north   south

Challenge

Circle your favorite animal on the map.

In which continent is it found?

____

A Land and Water Map of Colorado

Monday

1. The map shows ________.

   Arizona   Colorado

2. The map shows land and ________.

   cities   water

Tuesday

1. Which symbol stands for a mountain?

2. Which symbol stands for plains?

Wednesday

1. What is very high land?

2. What is low, flat land?

Daily Geography

A Land and Water Map of Colorado

WEEK 15

Thursday

1. The Great Plains are in the ________.

   east west

2. The Rocky Mountains are in the ________.

   east west

Friday

1. Which river is in the south?

   Rio Grande South Platte River

2. Which river has the same name as the state?

   Arkansas River Colorado River

Challenge

1. Color the mountains brown.
2. Color the plains green.
3. Color the rivers blue.

Daily Geography

WEEK 16

A Land and Water Map of Arizona

Monday

1. The map shows ________.

   Arizona   California

2. The map shows land and ________.

   cities   water

Tuesday

1. Which symbol stands for desert?  

2. Which symbol stands for canyon?  

Wednesday

1. Which desert is in the south?

   Painted Desert   Sonoran Desert

2. The Grand Canyon is in the ________.

   north   south

A Land and Water Map of Arizona

WEEK 16

Thursday

1. The ________ River runs through the Grand Canyon.

   Colorado Gila

2. The ________ is near the Sonoran Desert.

   Colorado River Gila River

Friday

1. Canyons, deserts, and mountains are ________.

   land water

2. Rivers are ________.

   land water

Challenge

1. Color the Grand Canyon red, yellow, and brown.
2. Color the Painted Desert and Sonoran Desert yellow.
3. Color the mountains brown.
4. Color the rivers blue.

A Land and Water Map of Hawaii

Monday

1. The map shows the ________ Island.

   Big Little

2. The map shows one island in ________.

   Hawaii California

Tuesday

1. Which symbol stands for ocean?  

2. Which symbol stands for waterfall?  

Wednesday

1. Which symbol stands for volcano?  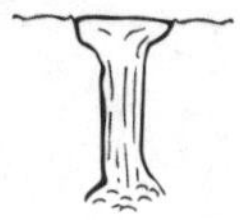

2. A volcano is a kind of ________.

   mountain river

Daily Geography

A Land and Water Map of Hawaii

WEEK 17

Thursday

1. There are waterfalls in the ________.

   north   south

2. There are ________ volcanoes on the island.

   3   5

Friday

1. Lava spills out of a ________.

   volcano   waterfall

2. Which ocean borders the island of Hawaii?

   ____

Challenge

1. Color the volcanoes black and red.
2. Color the waterfalls dark blue.
3. Color the rest of the island green.
4. Color the Pacific Ocean light blue.

Daily Geography

WEEK 18

A Land and Water Map of Oregon

Monday

1. The map shows ________.

   Hawaii Oregon

2. The map shows land and ________.

   cities water

Tuesday

1. Which symbol stands for forest?  

2. Which symbol stands for lake?  

Wednesday

1. Which symbol stands for mountain?  

2. How many mountains are named on the map?

   2 3 4

Daily Geography

WEEK 18

A Land and Water Map of Oregon

Thursday

1. Which river borders Oregon on the north?

   Willamette River   Columbia River

2. Which ocean borders Oregon on the west?

   Pacific Ocean   Atlantic Ocean

Friday

1. Which lake is in the Cascade Mountains?

   Crater Lake   Harney Lake

2. How much of Oregon is covered in forests?

   all   half

Challenge

1. Color the mountains brown.
2. Color the forests green.
3. Color the lakes dark blue.
4. Color the rivers light blue.

A Farm Map

Monday

1. The map shows a ________.

   farm   park

2. The farm is in the ________.

   countryside   town

Tuesday

1. The farm has a house and a ________.

   barn   store

2. The farmer uses a truck and a ________.

   bus   tractor

Wednesday

1. The farmer raises ________.

   cows   pigs

2. The farm is ________.

   on Rural Route 1   in Springville

Daily Geography

WEEK 19

A Farm Map

Thursday

1. Which road goes into town?

   Rural Route 1 County Home Road

2. Springville is ________ miles north of the farm.

   1 2 3

Friday

1. The farm is in a ________.

   rural area town

2. A rural area has a lot of ________.

   land people

Challenge

1. Where would you like to live?

   on a farm in a city

2. What is your favorite part of the farm?
   Finish the sentence on the map.

Daily Geography

WEEK 20

A Town Map

Monday

1. The map shows a ________.

   farm   town

2. The name of the town is ________.

   Oak Town   Youngtown

Tuesday

1. Where do people live?

   houses   school

2. Where do children play?

   bank   park

Wednesday

1. People ________ at the gas station.

   work   play

2. What is on Park Street?

   hospital   post office

Daily Geography

A Town Map

WEEK 20

Thursday

1. What is on Oak Street?

   fire station   gas station

2. What is not on Second Street?

   bank   park

Friday

1. Which road is west of Youngtown?

   Highway 1   Second Street

2. Which one has more people?

   farm   town

Challenge

1. Color one place to live in Youngtown yellow.
2. Color one place to play in Youngtown green.
3. Color one place to work in Youngtown red.

Daily Geography

WEEK 21

A City Map

Monday

1. The map shows a ________.

   big city small town

2. The name of the city is ________.

   Bank City Central City

Tuesday

1. There are a lot of ________ buildings in a city.

   red tall

2. The buildings in a city are ________ each other.

   close to far from

Wednesday

1. There is a car, a truck, and a ________ on the streets.

   bus train

2. People live in the ________.

   City Museum Garden Apartments

A City Map

Thursday

1. What is on First Street?

   City Museum   City Park

2. The bus stop is on ________.

   First Street   Park Avenue

Friday

1. Which one has more people?

   city   farm   town

2. The city has very tall buildings called ________.

   skyscrapers   museums

Challenge

1. Color your favorite place in Central City.
2. Would you like to live in Central City?
   Circle your answer on the map.

A State Map

Monday

1. The map shows ________.

   California   Texas

2. Texas is a ________.

   city   state

Tuesday

1. Which symbol stands for a city?   ✪   ◉

2. A ✪ stands for a ________.

   capital   city

Wednesday

1. The capital of Texas is ________.

   Austin   Dallas

2. What shows the border around Texas?

   ◉   – – – –

A State Map

Thursday

1. Which city is in the south?

   Amarillo Brownsville

2. Which city is west of Austin?

   El Paso Houston

Friday

1. Texas is in the ________ part of the United States.

   north south

2. Texas is one of the ________ states.

   larger smaller

Challenge

1. Color the capital yellow.
2. Color the city of Dallas blue.
3. Trace the border of Texas in green.

A Zoo Map

Monday

1. The map shows Central City ______.

   Park   Zoo

2. How many kinds of animals are on the map key?

   ____

Tuesday

1. Which symbol stands for lions?  

2. Which symbol stands for elephants?  

Wednesday

1. Which symbol stands for zebras?  

2. 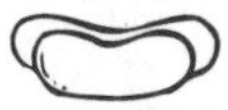 stands for ______.

   animals   food

A Zoo Map

Thursday

1. What is south of the Snack Shack?

   bears monkeys

2. What is north and west of the Snack Shack?

   lions zebras

Friday

1. What is east of the Animal Path?

   elephants lions

2. Wild Way runs ________.

   east and west north and south

Challenge

1. Color the zoo animals at Central City Zoo.
2. Which zoo animal is your favorite?
   Write its name on the map.

A Fun Park Map

Monday

1. The map shows a ________.

   fun park petting zoo

2. What is at Wild World Park?

   animals rides

Tuesday

1. How many rides are there?

   3 6

2. One of the rides is a ________.

   Ferris wheel Rocket

Wednesday

1. Where can you eat?

   Log Ride Snack Shack

2. What is next to the Snack Shack?

   Merry-Go-Round Train

A Fun Park Map

Thursday

1. Which ride gets you wet?

    Log Ride   Train Ride

2. The clown is next to the ________.

    gift shop   restrooms

Friday

1. You enter the park at the ________ end.

    north   south

2. What is near the exit?

    Bumper Cars   Ferris wheel

Challenge

1. Color your favorite ride at the fun park.
2. Write which ride you like best on the map.

A Weather Map

Monday

1. What kind of map is it?

   land and water map   weather map

2. The weather map shows ________ states.

   5   6

Tuesday

1. Which symbol stands for sunny?

2. Which symbol stands for partly cloudy?

Wednesday

1. Which symbol stands for snow?

2. South Dakota is having ________.

   rain   snow

A Weather Map

Thursday

1. What is the weather in North Dakota?

   rainy snowy

2. What is the weather in Iowa?

   partly cloudy sunny

Friday

1. Nebraska and South Dakota have ________.

   clouds rain

2. Which season of the year is it?

   summer winter

Challenge

1. Color one state that has your favorite kind of weather.
2. Finish the sentences on the map.

A Desert Habitat

Monday

1. The map shows a ________.

    desert   forest

2. The map shows a ________ desert.

    cold   hot

Tuesday

1. A ________ is an animal on the map.

    snake   cactus

2. A ________ is a plant on the map.

    lizard   cactus

Wednesday

1. A desert has rocks and ________.

    grass   sand

2. The air is hot and ________.

    wet   dry

A Desert Habitat

Thursday

1. What is in the north part of the desert?

   mountains rivers

2. Adobe houses help people stay ________.

   cool warm

Friday

1. A habitat is ________.

   a home an animal

2. A desert habitat is for ________.

   only plants animals, plants, and people

Challenge

Here are more desert animals.

coyote	jackrabbit	kangaroo rat
roadrunner	scorpion	tarantula

1. Choose one desert animal from the list.
2. Draw it on the map.

Daily Geography

WEEK 27

Moving to the City

Monday

1. The map shows a town and a ________.

   city   state

2. The Brown family is ________.

   moving   playing

Tuesday

1. The Brown family is leaving ________.

   Parker   Springville

2. The Brown family is moving to ________.

   Parker   Springville

Wednesday

1. Which one is a small town?

   Parker   Springville

2. Which one is a city?

   Parker   Springville

Daily Geography

Moving to the City

WEEK 27

Thursday

1. The moving van will go on Highway ______.

   1 3 5

2. How many people live in Springville?

   5,000 50,000

Friday

1. There are more people in ______.

   Parker Springville

2. Mr. and Mrs. Brown are moving because they have new ______.

   jobs cars

Challenge

Would you like to live in Springville or Parker?

1. Write which place you would like to live on the map.
2. Write its population.

Daily Geography

WEEK 28

A County Fair Map

Monday

1. The map shows a ________.

   farm　　　　county fair

2. The county fair is ________.

   inside　　　　outside

Tuesday

1. There are ________ animals at the fair.

   farm　　　　wild

2. There are ________ kinds of animals.

   4　　　　6

Wednesday

1. Which ride is at the county fair?

   Ferris wheel　　　　roller coaster

2. Name one kind of food sold at the fair.

   ____

A County Fair Map

Thursday

1. There are ________ in the arts and crafts area.

   games rugs

2. You can win a ________ at the fair.

   baseball hat teddy bear

Friday

1. A lady is ________ on the stage.

   eating singing

2. You enter the county fair at the ________ gate.

   north south

Challenge

1. Color your favorite area at the county fair.
2. Name your favorite area on the map.

A Supermarket Map

Monday

1. The map shows a ________.

   shoe store   supermarket

2. You can buy ________ at this supermarket.

   shoes   food

Tuesday

1. What is in aisle 1?

   canned foods   cereals

2. What is in aisle 2?

   canned foods   cereals

Wednesday

1. What is in aisle 3?

   dairy products   fruits and vegetables

2. What is next to the meat counter?

   bakery   check-out

A Supermarket Map

Thursday

1. The scale ________ the fruits and vegetables.

   counts   weighs

2. Which one is <u>not</u> in the dairy case?

   cake   butter   milk

Friday

1. Which one is a product in this supermarket?

   candy   check-out

2. Where do you pay for your food?

   bakery   check-out

Challenge

Color one product from each area of the supermarket.

Homes in a Community

Monday

1. The map shows ________ in a community.

   homes　　　　parks

2. All the homes are on ________.

   highways　　　　streets

Tuesday

1. Sweet Homes has ________ homes.

   3　　　　6

2. Honey Mobile Homes has ________ homes.

   2　　　　4

Wednesday

1. A ________ is two houses joined by a wall.

   duplex　　　　mobile home

2. Candy Lane has ________.

   apartments　　　　duplexes

Homes in a Community

Thursday

1. How many homes are on Duplex Row?

   4 6 8

2. ________ Homes is on Roll Street.

   Sugar Sweet

Friday

1. Which street runs north and south?

   Baker Street Cookie Street

2. What is east of Sugar Homes?

   park empty lot

Challenge

Draw your favorite kind of home on the map.

Daily Geography

Community Helpers

WEEK 31

Monday

1. The map shows the buildings where ________ work.

   community helpers   apartments

2. The map shows a ________ station.

   fire   gas

Tuesday

1. Where do you go if you are sick?

   hospital   post office

2. Where do you go to learn?

   hospital   school

Wednesday

1. Where can you check out books?

   library   post office

2. Where do you mail a letter?

   library   post office

Community Helpers

Thursday

1. A ________ takes children to school.

   bus truck

2. A ________ uses a siren.

   fire truck school bus

Friday

1. Community helpers work ________.

   alone together

2. What is used for an emergency?

   dump truck ambulance

Challenge

Which community helper would you like to be?

bus driver	firefighter	mail carrier	police officer
doctor	librarian	nurse	teacher

1. Circle one community helper.
2. Color the place where you would work on the map.

Farms in Iowa

Monday

1. The map shows the state of ________.

    Iowa   Texas

2. There are 87,000 ________ in Iowa.

    farms   ranches

Tuesday

1. Which symbol stands for dairy cows?

2. Which symbol stands for soybeans?

Wednesday

1. Iowa grows the most ________.

    corn   hay

2. Corn and ________ are plants.

    hogs   soybeans

Farms in Iowa

Thursday

1. Iowa raises the most ________.

   ducks hogs

2. Dairy cows and hogs are ________.

   animals plants

Friday

1. Iowa is number 8 in the United States for ________.

   dairy cows beef cattle

2. Dairy cows give us ________.

   eggs milk

Challenge

1. Pretend you are a farmer.
2. Choose one animal to raise.
3. Color the animal on the map.
4. Choose one plant to grow.
5. Color the plant on the map.

Visit California!

Monday

1. The map shows the state of ________.

   California Texas

2. What kind of map is shown?

   tourist map weather map

Tuesday

1. A tourist is a person who ________.

   farms travels

2. California borders the ________ Ocean.

   Atlantic Pacific

Wednesday

1. What can you see in Anaheim?

   Disneyland Mojave Desert

2. Which city is Hollywood in?

   Los Angeles San Francisco

Daily Geography

Visit California!

WEEK 33

Thursday

1. Where can you see lions?

   Monterey Bay Aquarium San Diego Zoo

2. ________ is a very hot place in California.

   Lake Tahoe Mojave Desert

Friday

1. ________ National Park is in the north part of the state.

   Redwood Yosemite

2. What islands can you visit in California?

   ____

Challenge

Be a tourist in California!

1. Choose your favorite place to visit. Color it on the map.
2. Name your favorite place on the map.

Natural Resources of Alaska

Monday

1. The map shows the state of ________.

   Alaska California

2. Which city is the capital of Alaska?

   Anchorage Juneau

Tuesday

1. Which symbol stands for gold?  

2. There are ________ areas where gold is found.

   2 4

Wednesday

1. Which symbol stands for lumber?  

2. What is found in the Pacific Ocean?  

Natural Resources of Alaska

Thursday

1. Lumber comes from ______.

   trees   fish

2. Which city is in the north?

   Barrow   Fairbanks

Friday

1. Which natural resource is near Anchorage?

   oil   gold

2. Natural resources are found ______.

   only in water   only on land   in water and on land

Challenge

1. Color the oil black.
2. Color the gold yellow.
3. Color the lumber brown.
4. Color the crab red.
5. Color the fish pink.
6. Color the oceans blue.

A Frontier Town

Monday

1. The map shows a ______.

    frontier town   city

2. The map shows how a town looked ______.

    long ago   today

Tuesday

1. The map shows a ______.

    hotel   hospital

2. Where did people go to buy things?

    General Store   Pony Express

Wednesday

1. The blacksmith worked in a ______.

    barn   hotel

2. The pony express delivered ______.

    food   mail

Daily Geography

A Frontier Town

WEEK 35

Thursday

1. People traveled on ________.

   airplanes horses

2. Who makes horseshoes?

   blacksmith sheriff

Friday

1. The map shows a town 150 ________ ago.

   days years

2. Which buildings have the same names that we use today?

   bank and hotel blacksmith and general store

Challenge

Pretend you live in this frontier town. What would you like to do? Write your answer on the map.

A Neighborhood Plan

Monday

1. The map shows a ________.

   big city   neighborhood

2. There are ________ houses in the neighborhood.

   4   6

Tuesday

1. The houses are on Lily Lane and ________.

   Center Street   Rose Avenue

2. Garden Elementary is a ________.

   bus stop   school

Wednesday

1. Where can people go to get gas?

   Garden Elementary   Quick Stop

2. What is south of the Quick Stop?

   bus stop   flag

A Neighborhood Plan

Daily Geography

WEEK 36

Thursday

1. Which street runs north and south?

   Center Street　　　Rose Avenue

2. What is north of Lily Lane?

   empty lot　　　houses

Friday

1. Which one is the smallest area?

   a city　　　a neighborhood　　　a state

2. What is a piece of land called that has <u>not</u> been used?

   a farm　　　an empty lot

Challenge

What would you build on the empty lot? Make a plan. Draw it on the map.

What Is a Map?

A map is a drawing of a place from above.

A map shows where things are.

This is a map of Joey's bedroom.

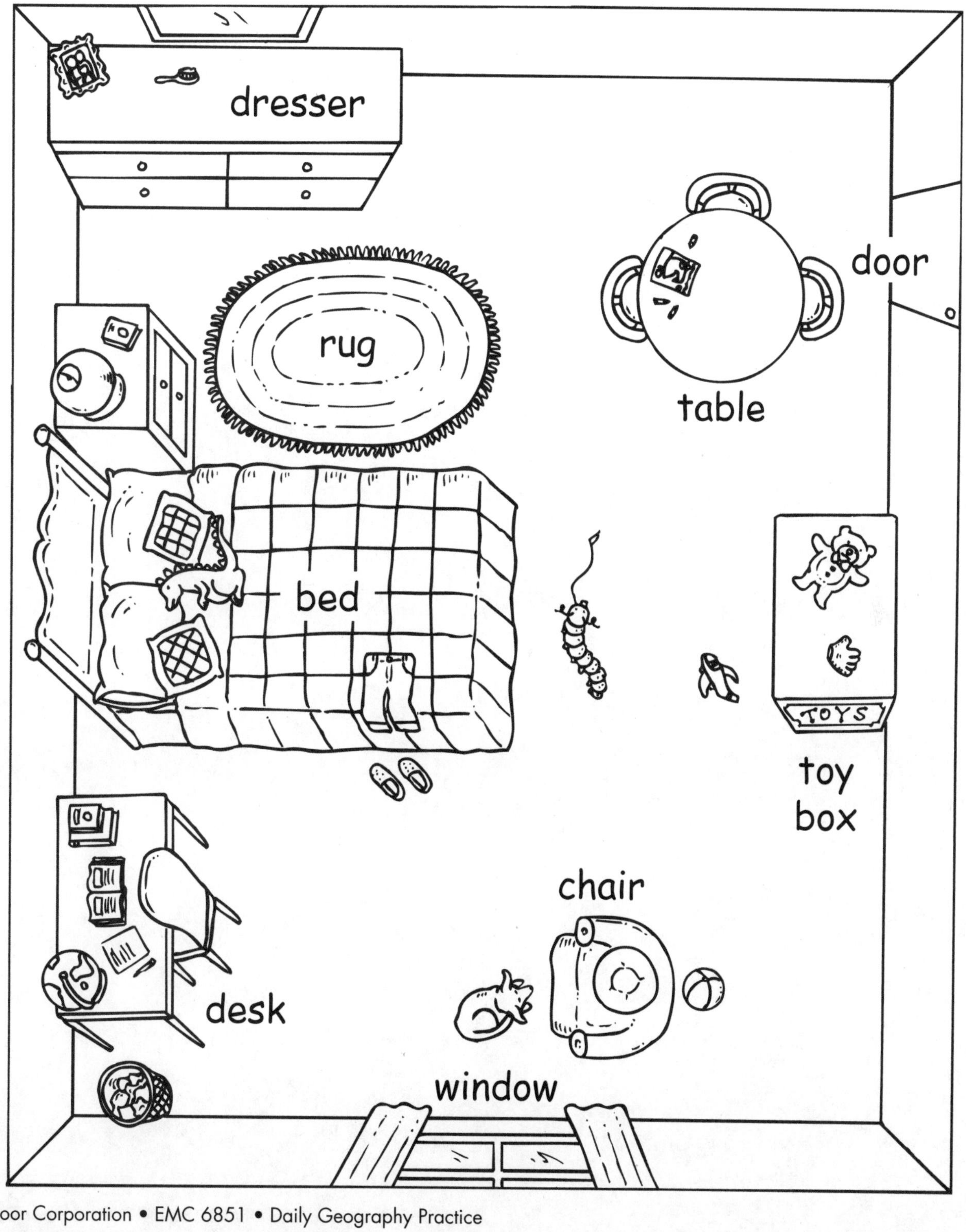

Using a Map

Mr. Brown's Classroom

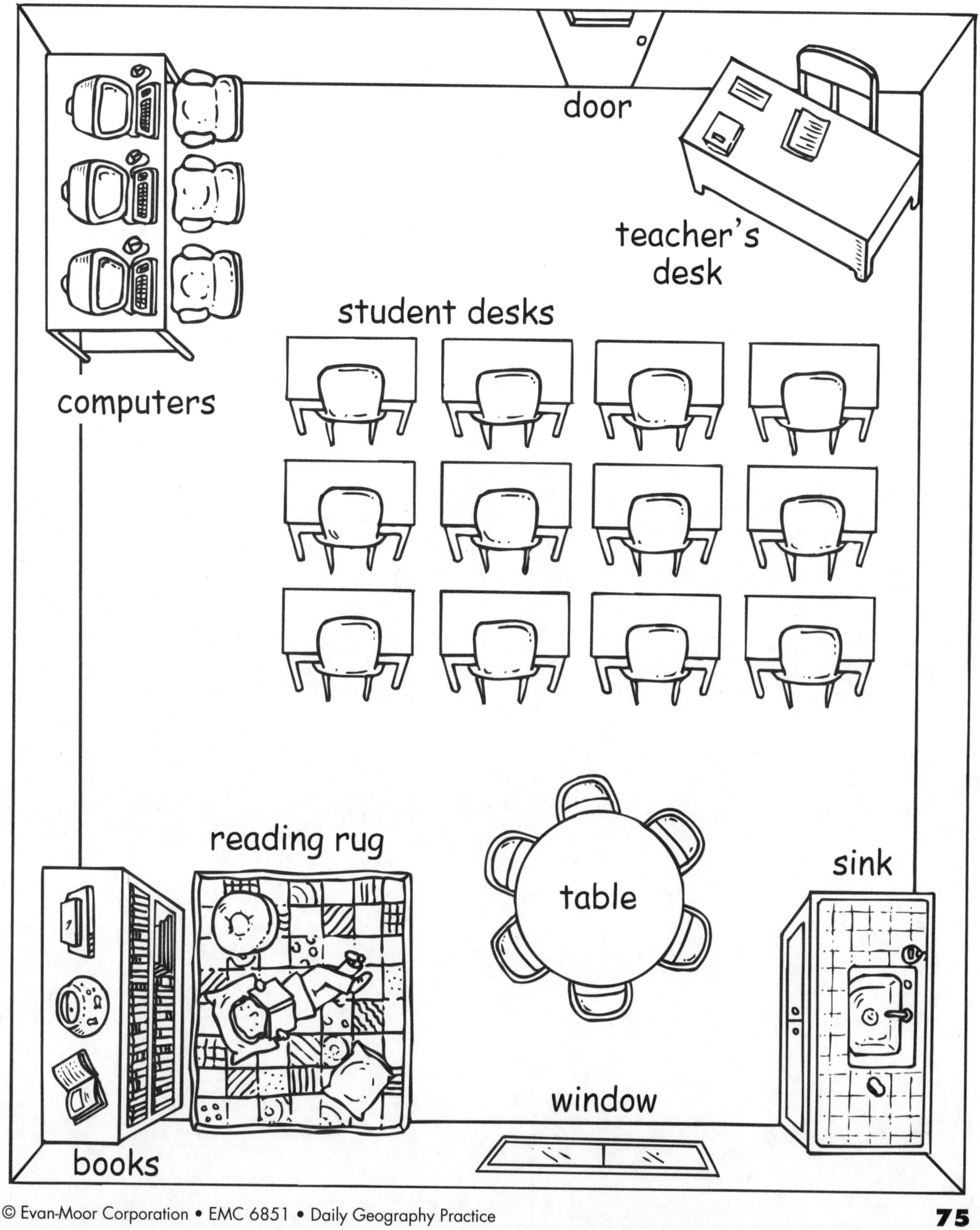

Finding Places on a Map

This map shows an apartment building.
Apartments are homes for people.
This map shows where people live.

Directions on a Map

This map shows a school. This map has directions on it. The directions are north, south, east, and west.

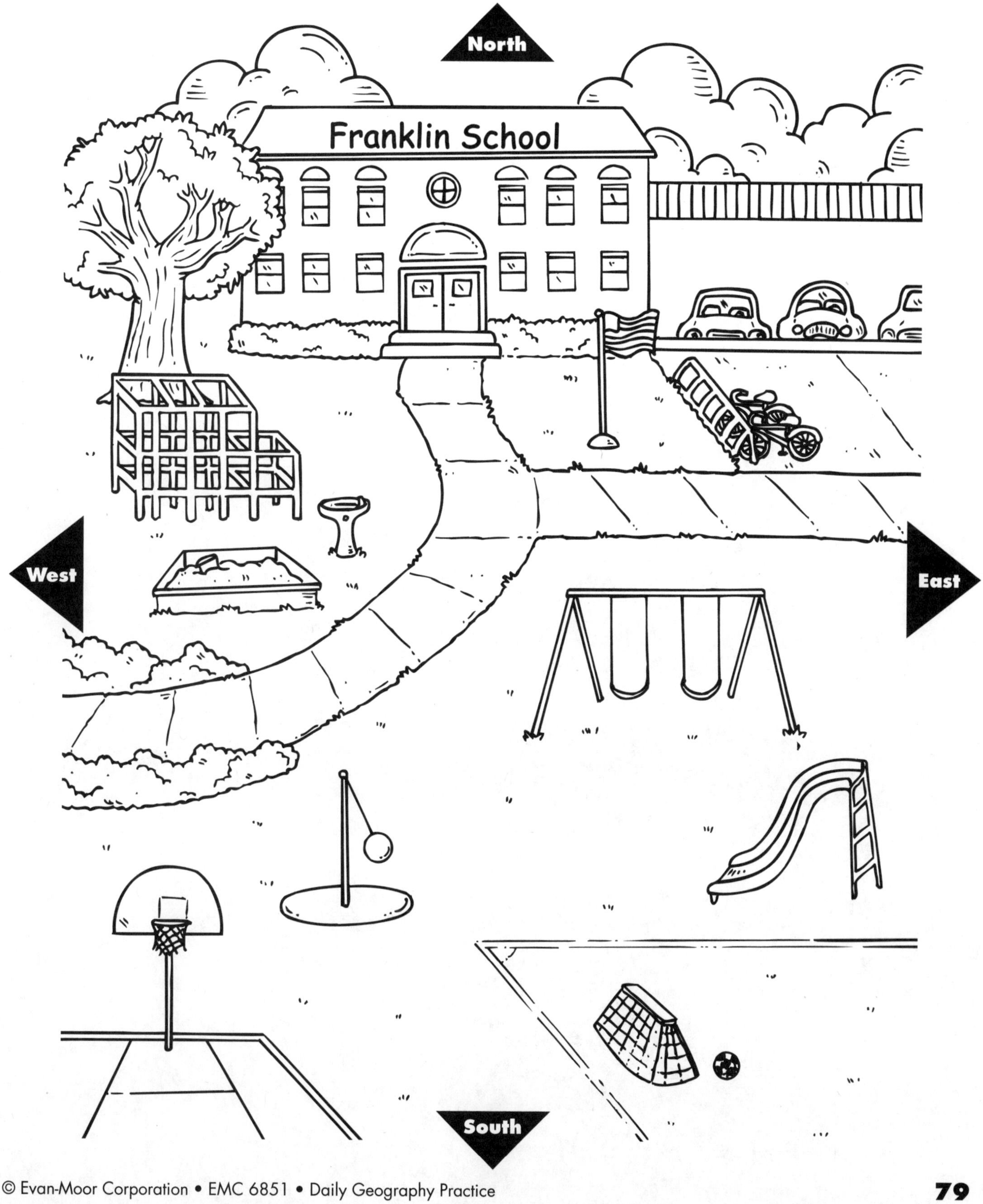

Using Directions

This is a compass rose.

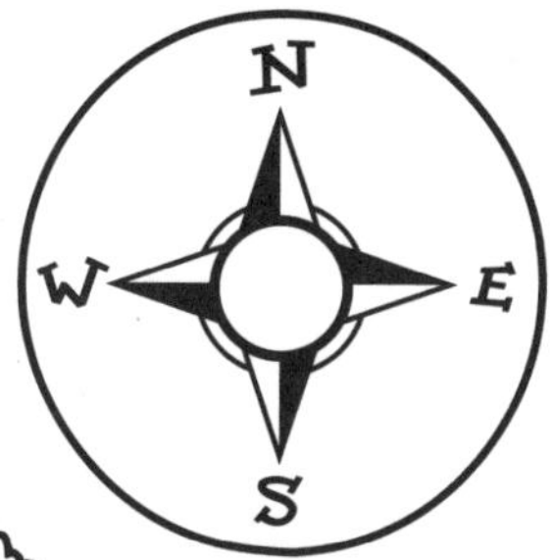

- The letter **N** stands for north.
- The letter **S** stands for south.
- The letter **E** stands for east.
- The letter **W** stands for west.

A Map Key

This map has a key. A map key has symbols.
The symbols are drawings. They stand for real things.

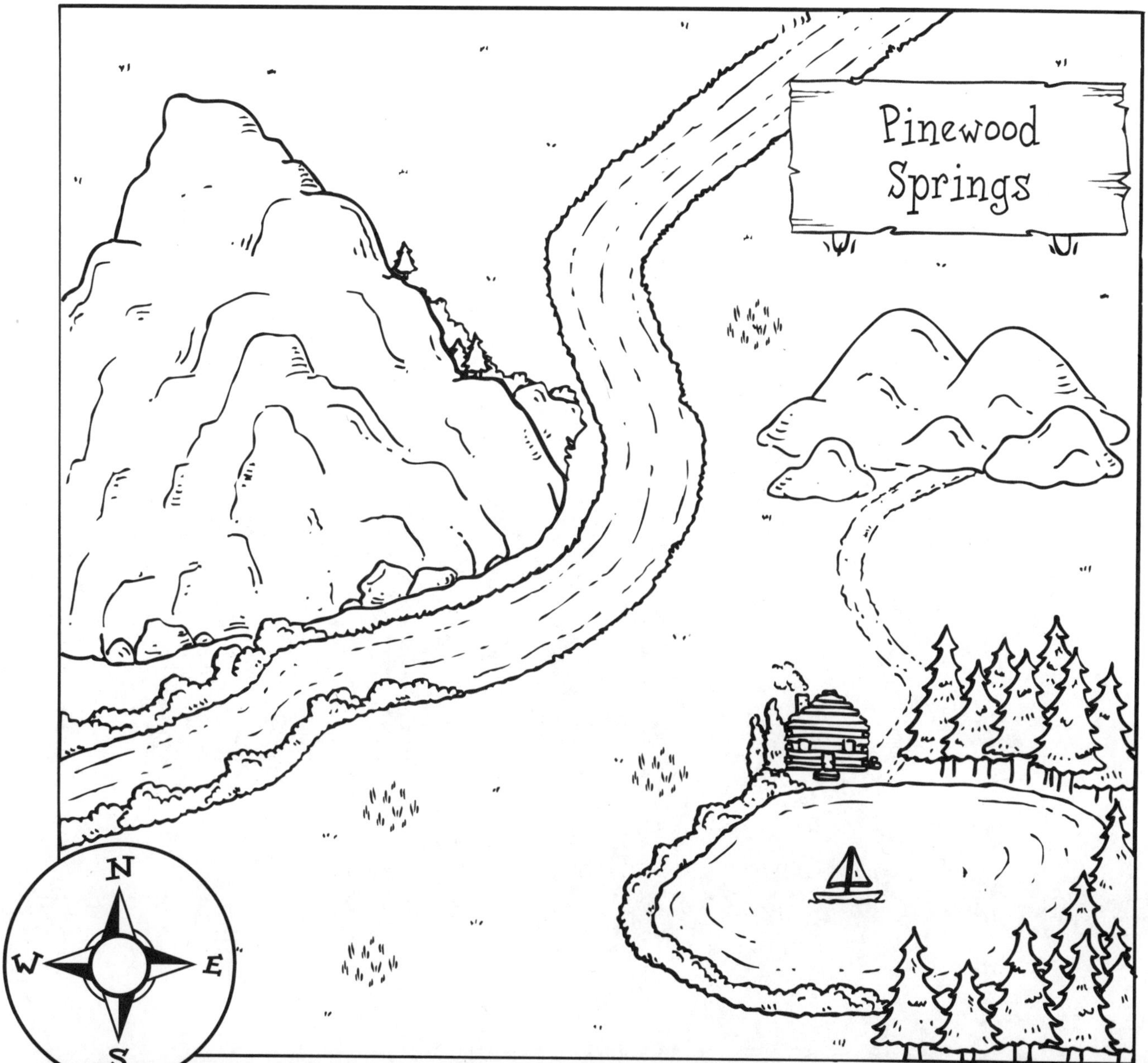

Map Key

mountain river hill
lake plain

Using a Map Key

This map has a key. A map key has symbols.
The symbols are drawings. They stand for real things.

Map Key

camp lake trail woods

Parts of a Map

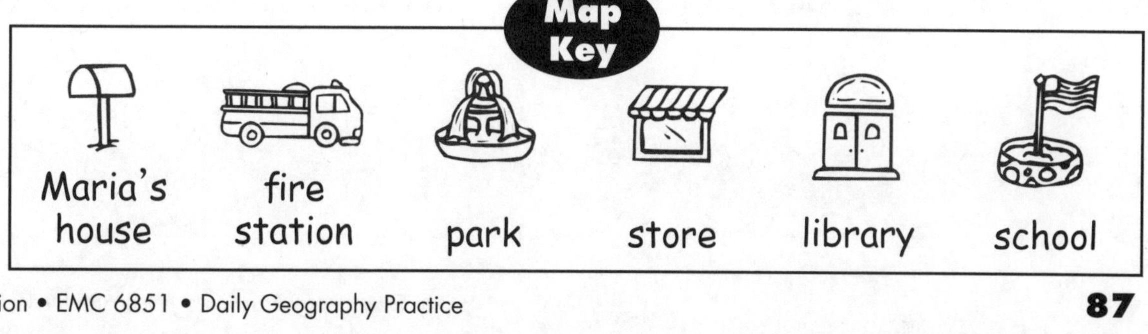

Picturing a Place

This is a map of Joey's backyard. Look at it for one minute. Now close your eyes. Think of Joey's backyard. Open your eyes. You made a picture in your mind.

Picturing the United States

The United States is a large country.
It has 50 states.

A Treasure Map

This is Pete's map.
He is looking for treasure.
Which way should he go?
Follow the route.

A Street Map

This is Kari's neighborhood. She wants to go to school. Which route should she take? Which way should she go?

What Is a Globe?

A globe is a model of Earth. It is round like Earth.

A globe shows the continents.
Continents are large areas of land.

A globe shows oceans. Oceans are large bodies of water.

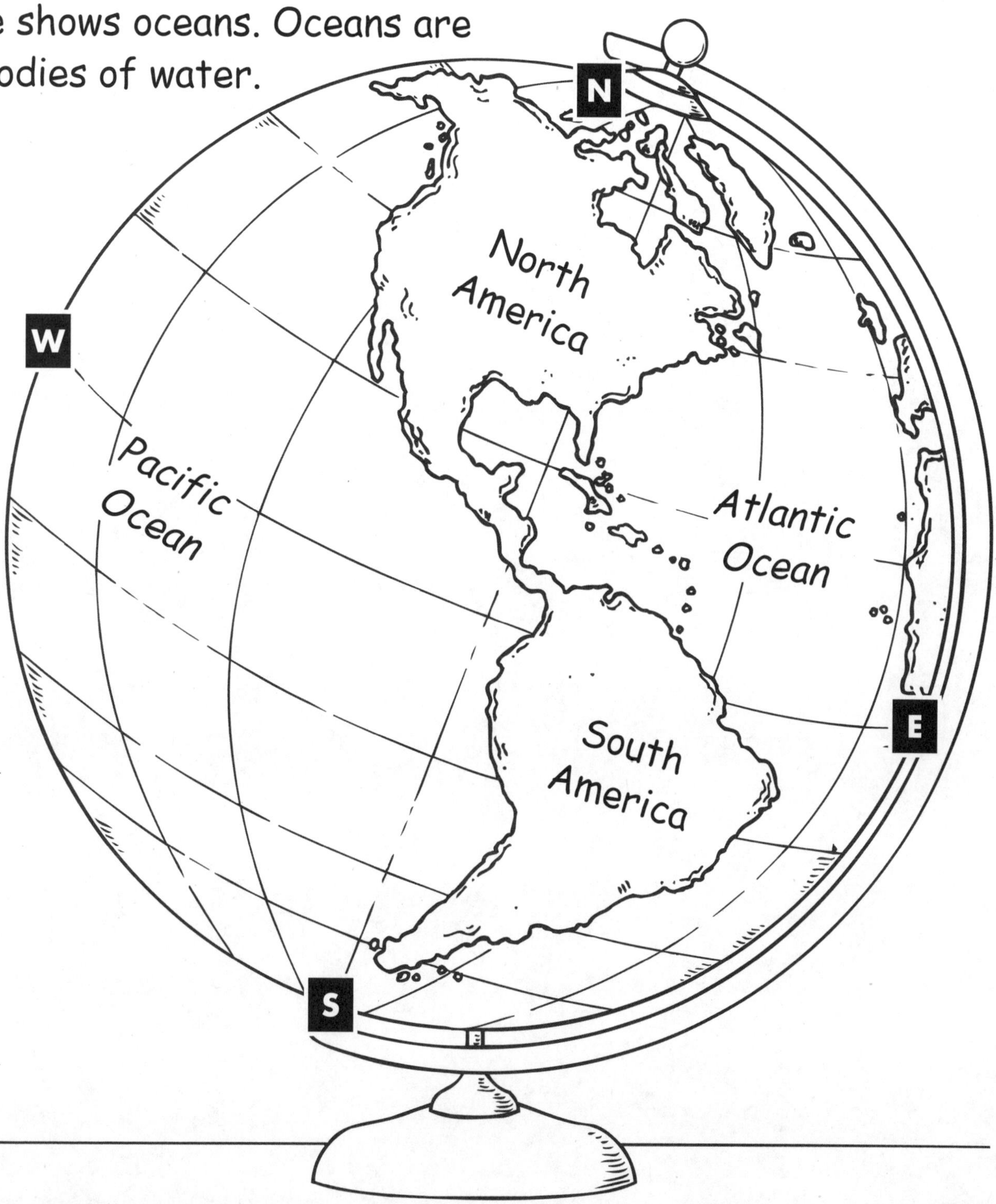

A World Map

The world has 7 large areas of land. They are called continents.
The world has 5 large bodies of water. They are called oceans.

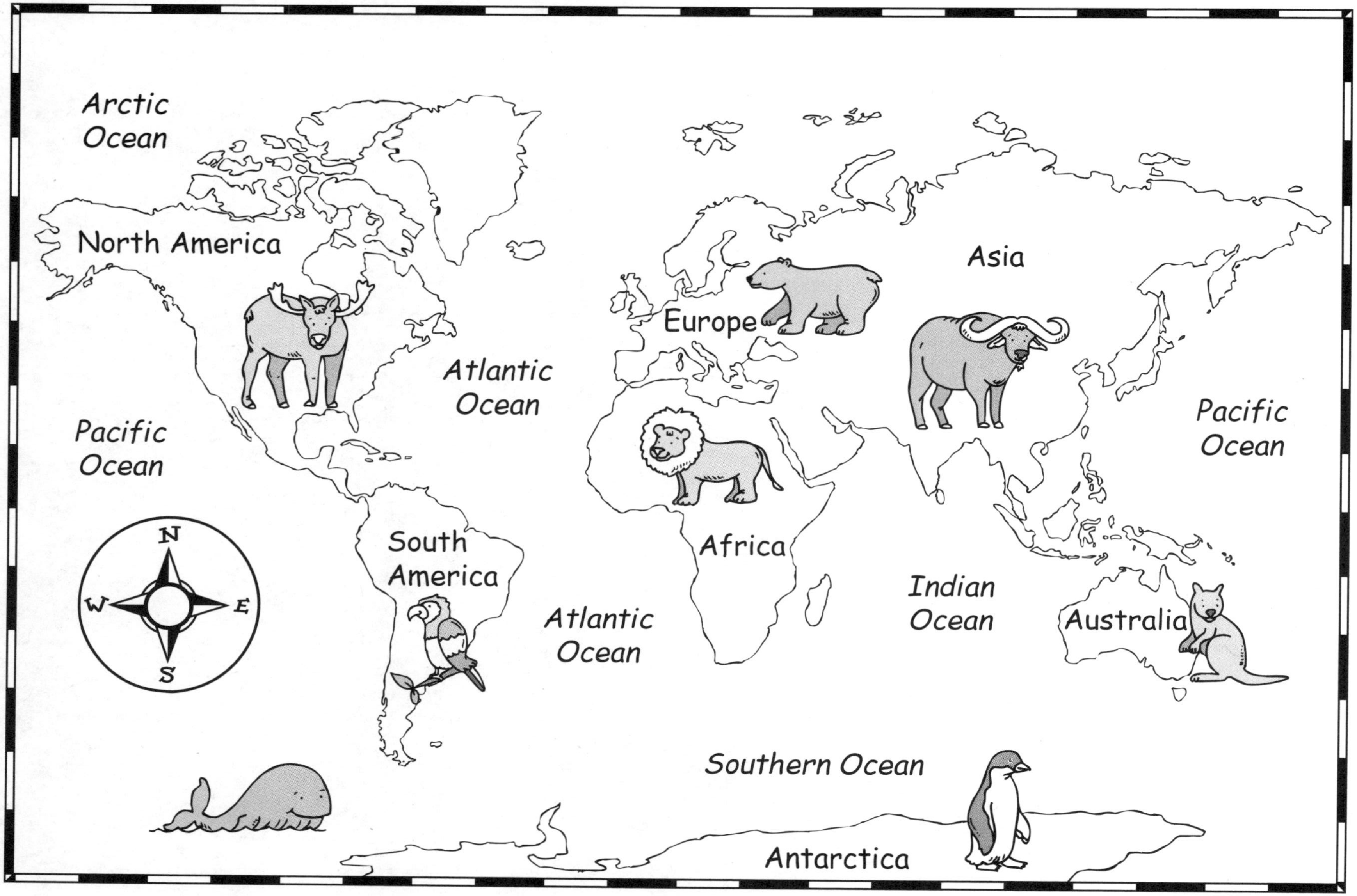

A Land and Water Map of Colorado

Colorado has many mountains. The mountains are very high land. Colorado has plains. The plains are very low, flat land.

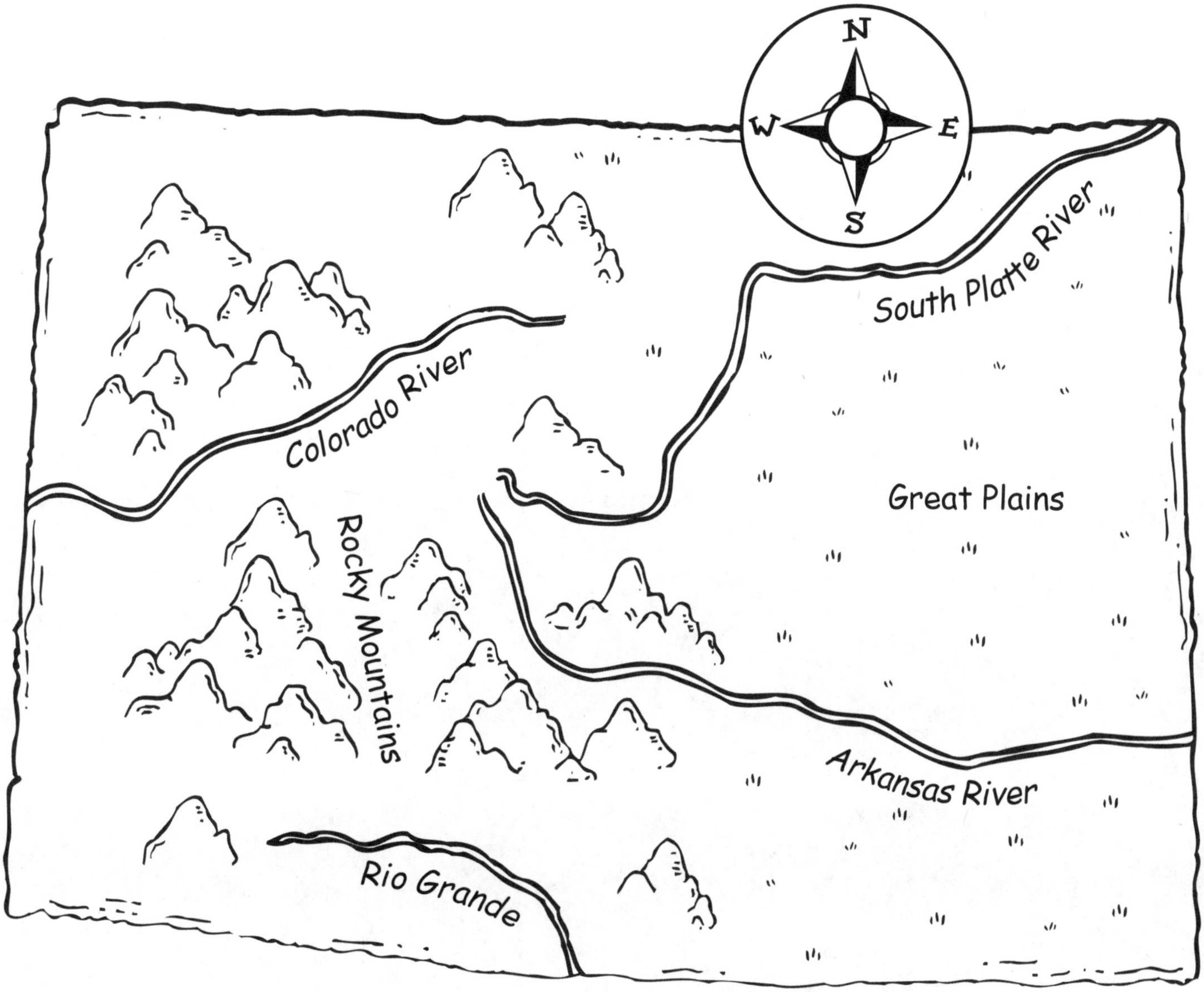

Map Key

A Land and Water Map of Arizona

Arizona has deserts. The deserts are hot and dry. They are sandy and rocky. Arizona has a large canyon. The canyon is a deep valley. It has steep sides.

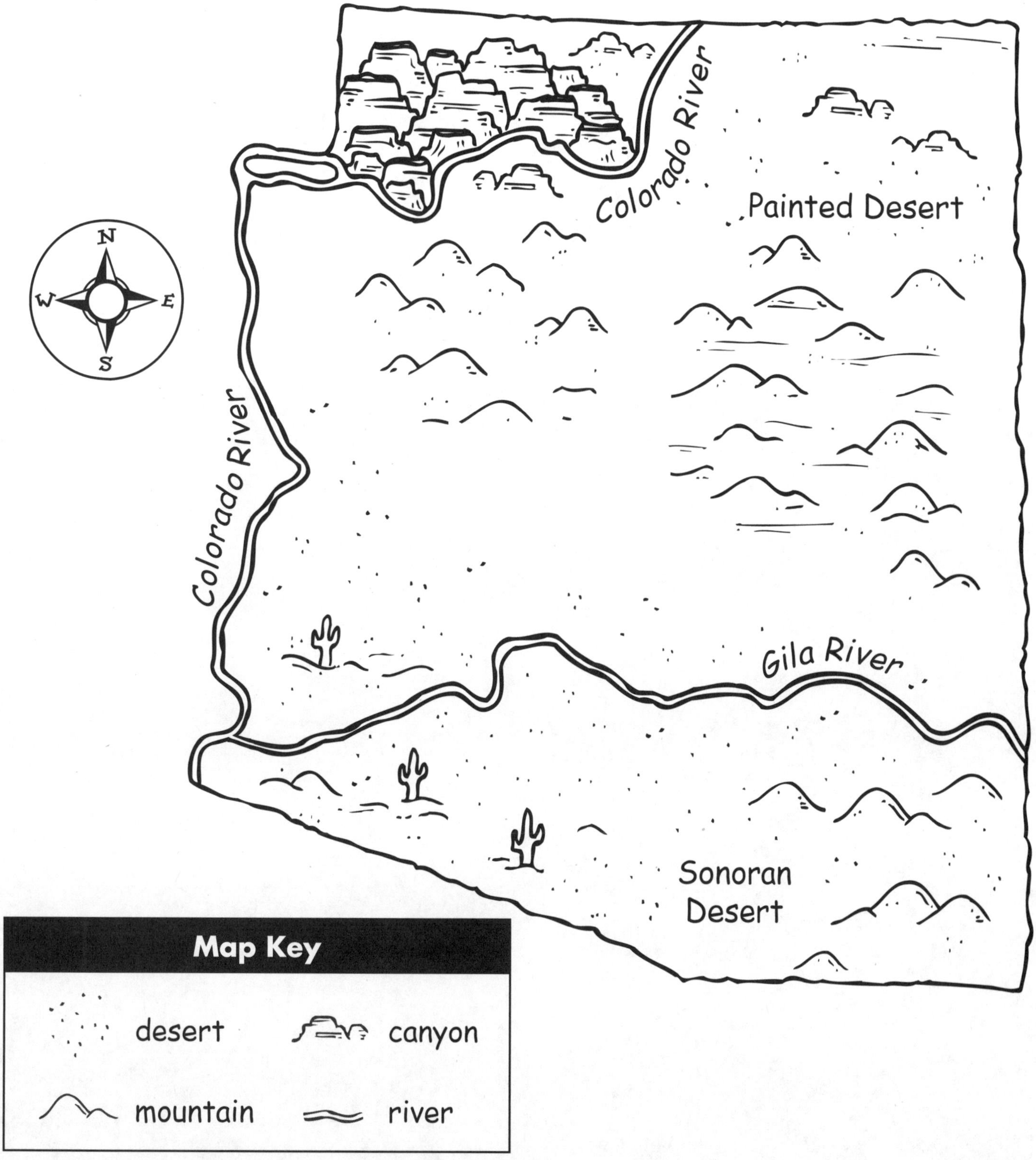

A Land and Water Map of Hawaii

This is one island in Hawaii. The island has volcanoes. A volcano is a mountain. It has an opening. Lava, ashes, and gases spill out. The island has waterfalls. A waterfall is a stream of water. The water falls from a high place.

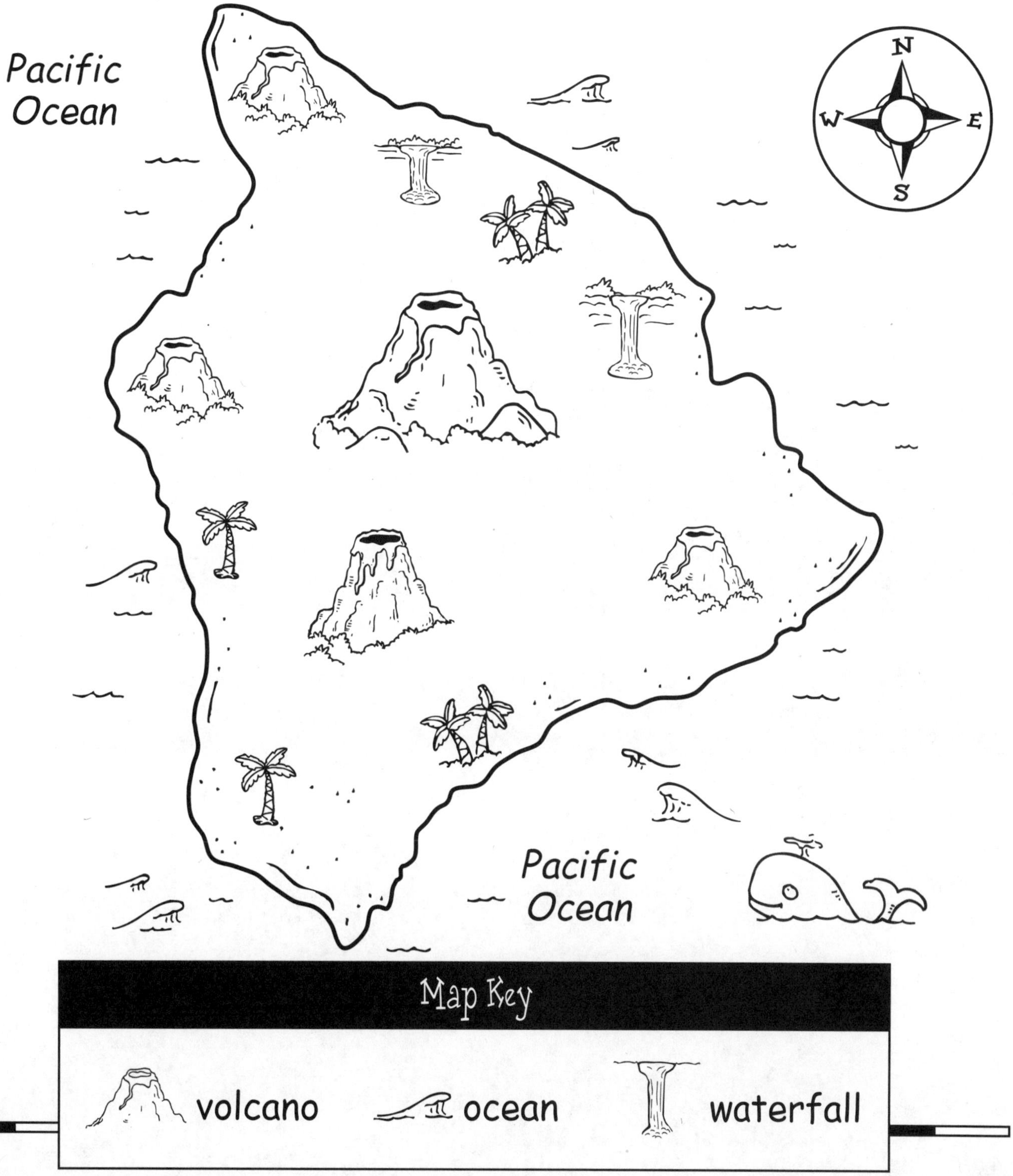

A Land and Water Map of Oregon

Half of Oregon is covered in forests. Oregon has large mountains. It has long rivers and deep lakes.

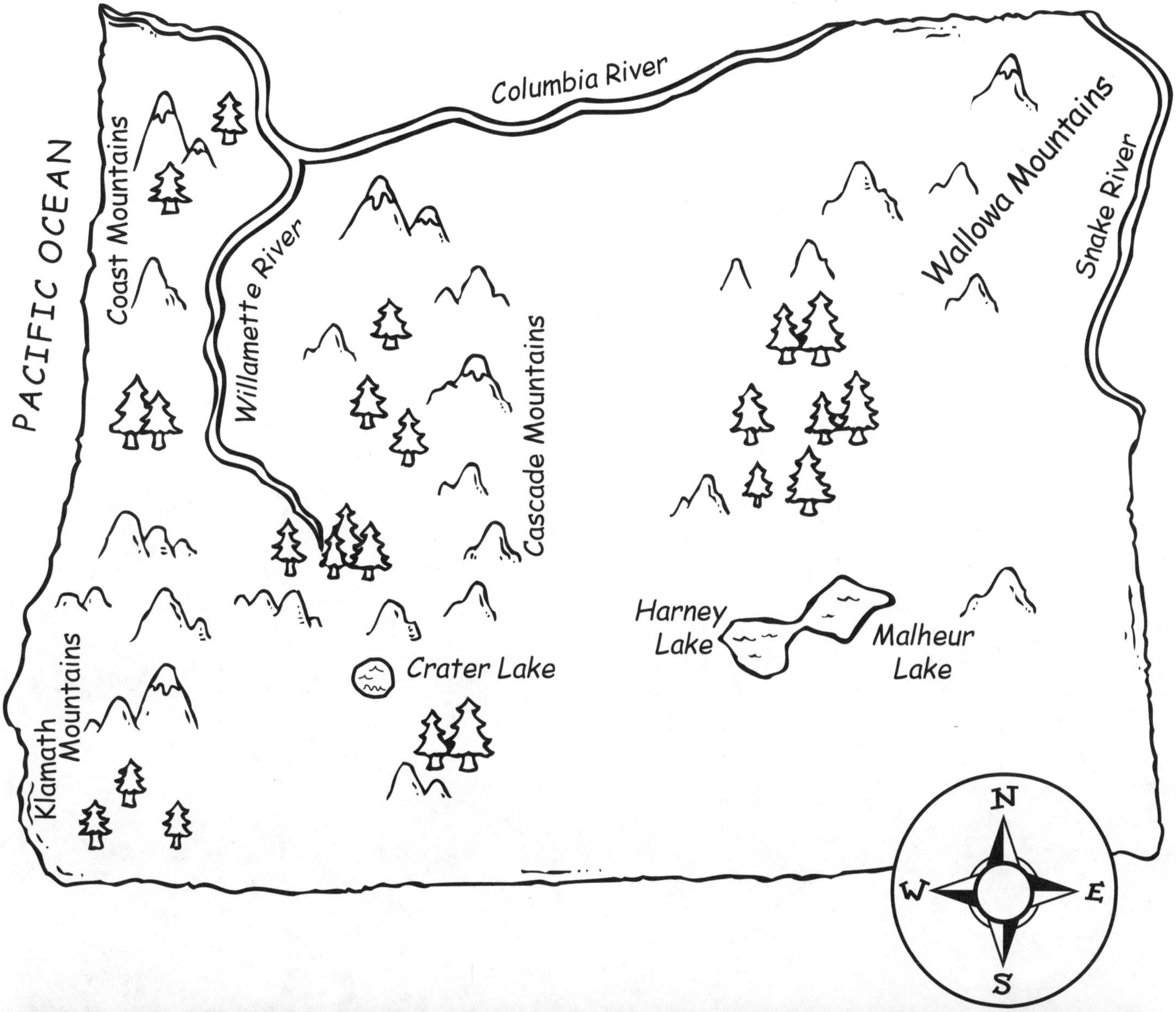

A Farm Map

A farm is in a rural area. It is in the countryside. There is a lot of land.

My favorite part of the farm is the ______________________.

A Town Map

This map shows Youngtown. People live, work, and play there.

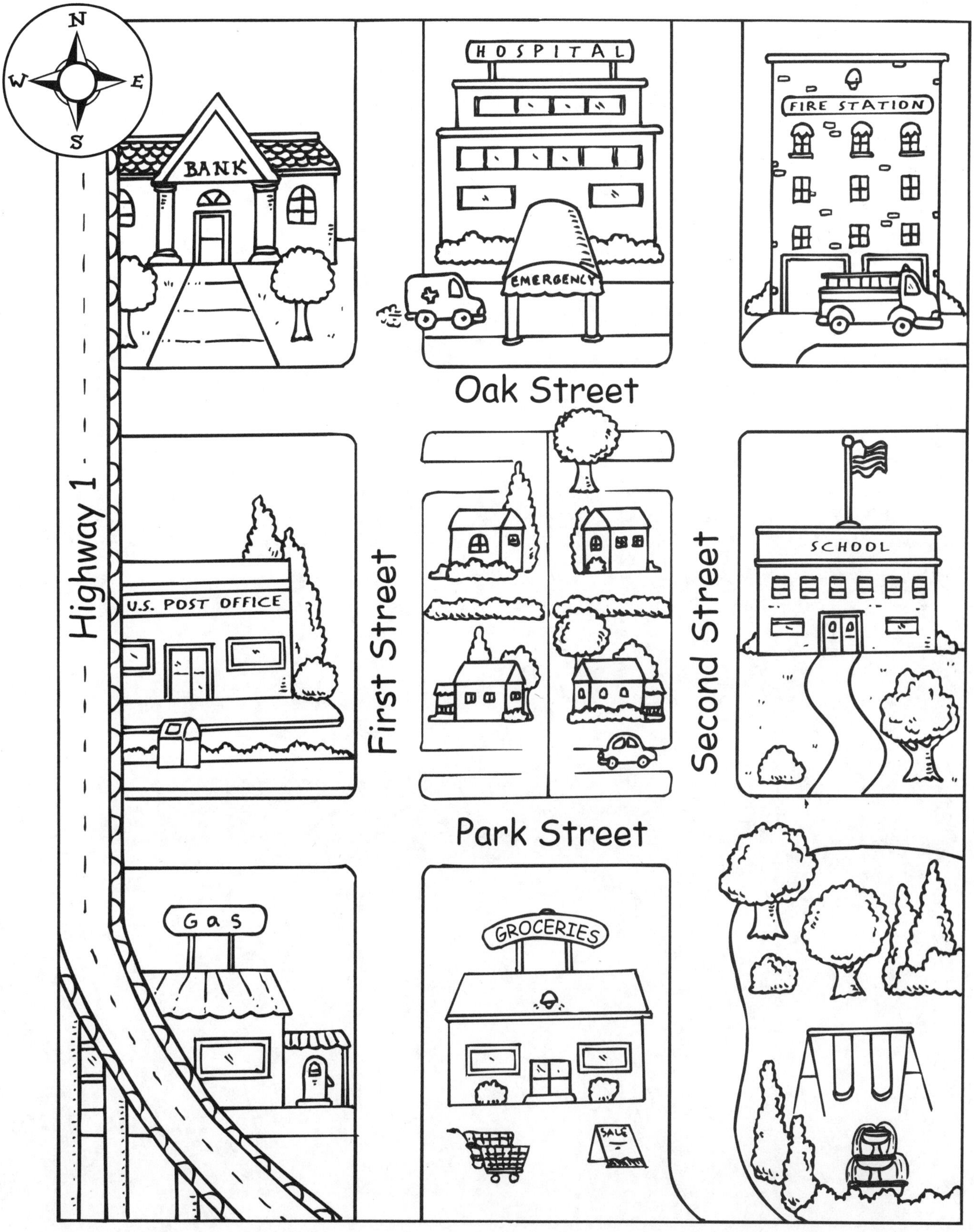

A City Map

This city is a very large town. It is a busy and crowded place. It has many tall buildings called skyscrapers.

Central City

Would you like to live in Central City? yes no

A State Map

This map shows Texas. Texas is a large state.
It is in the United States.

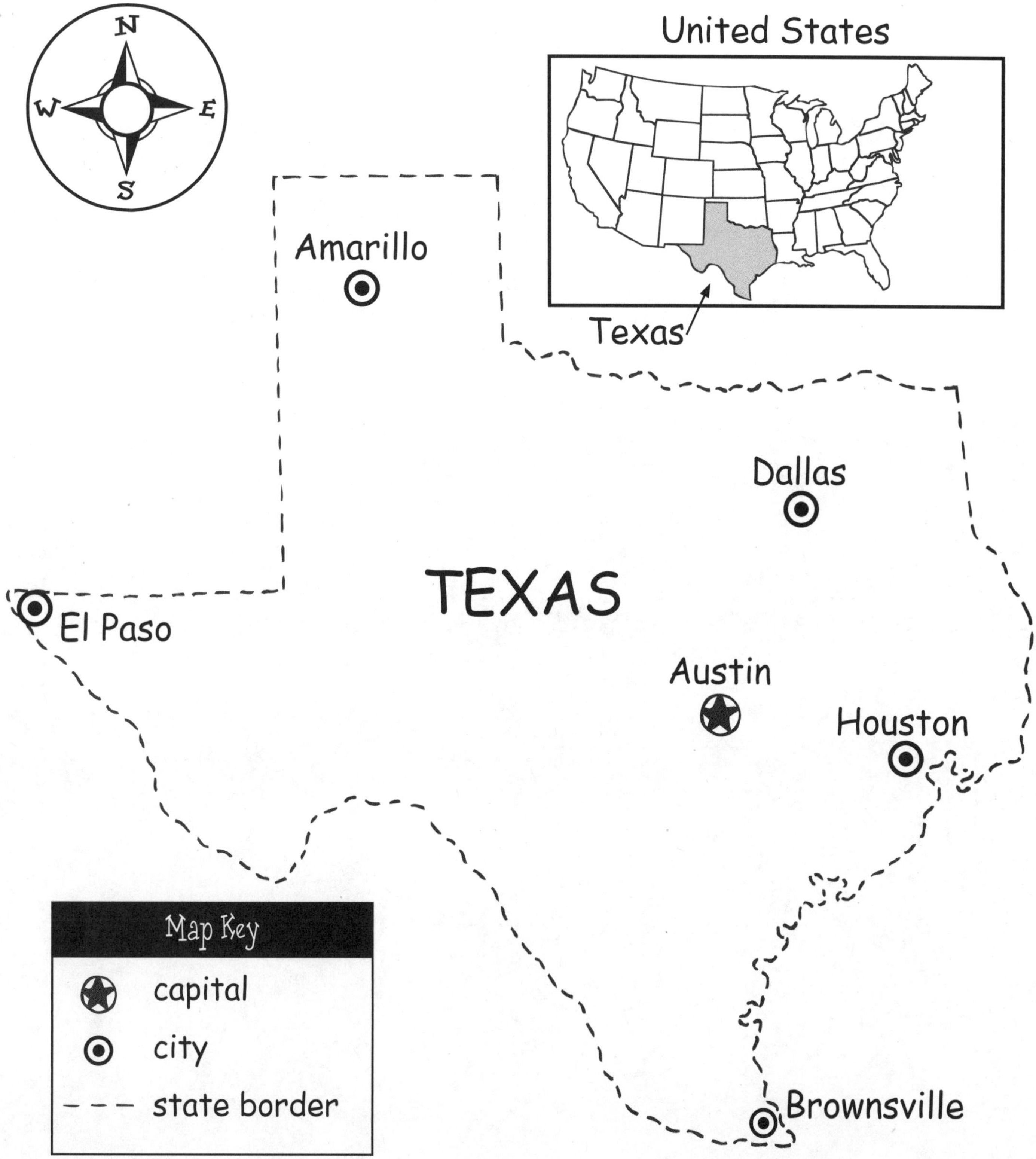

A Zoo Map

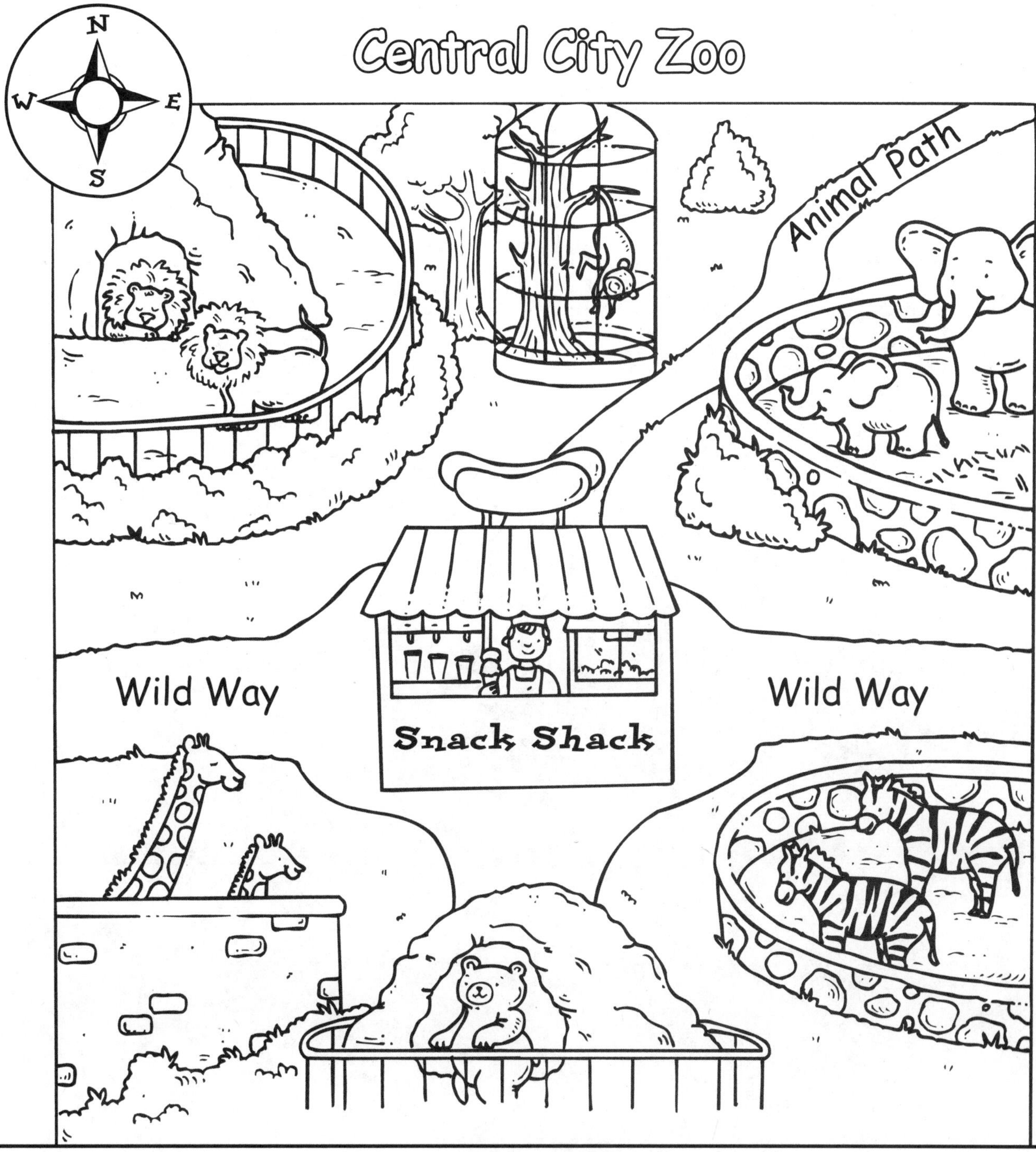

Map Key

Bears Giraffes Zebras Elephants
Lions Food Monkeys

Which zoo animal is your favorite? ______________________

A Fun Park Map

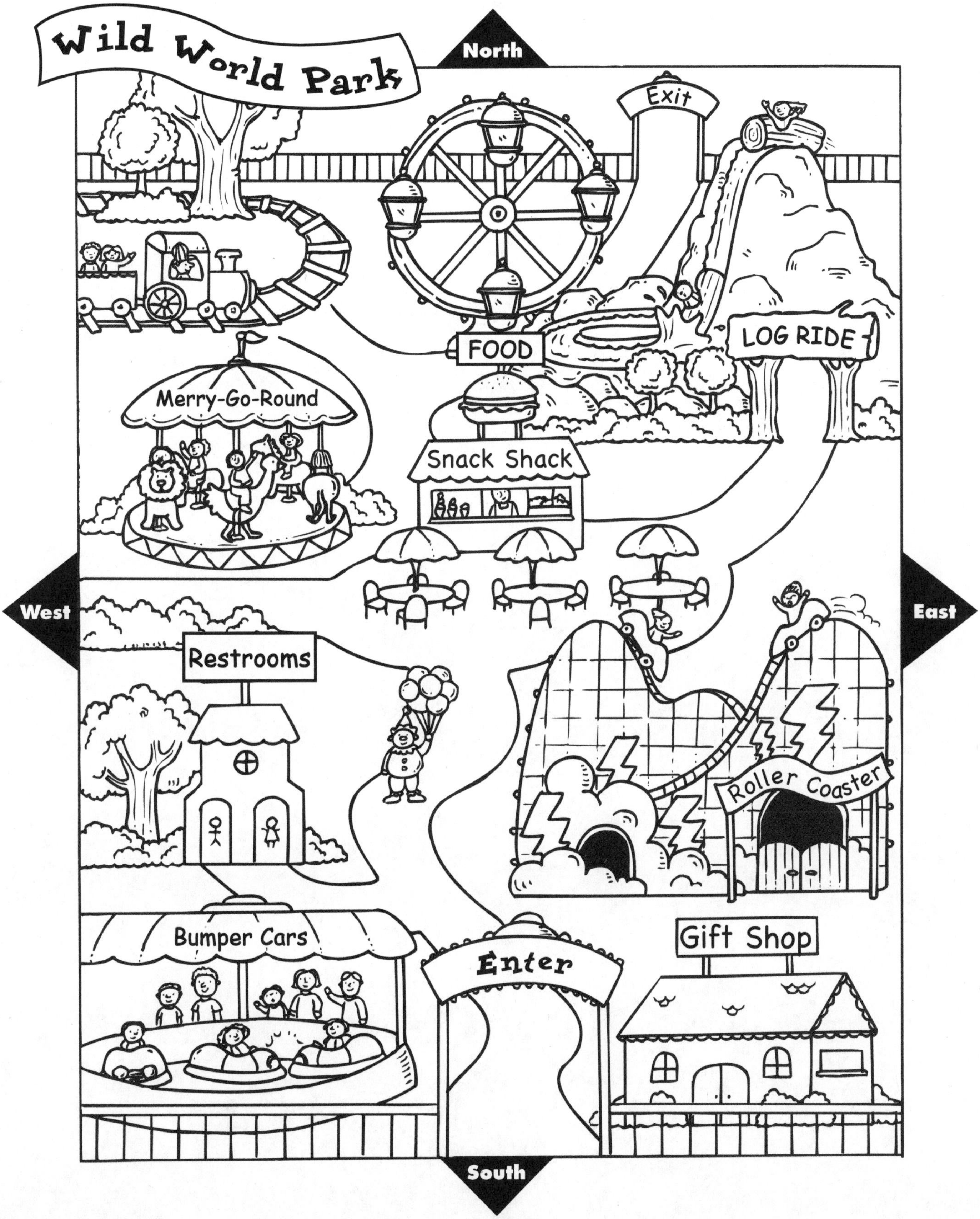

I like the ________________________________ the best.

A Weather Map

This map shows five states. It shows the weather in each state. The weather is what the air outside is like.

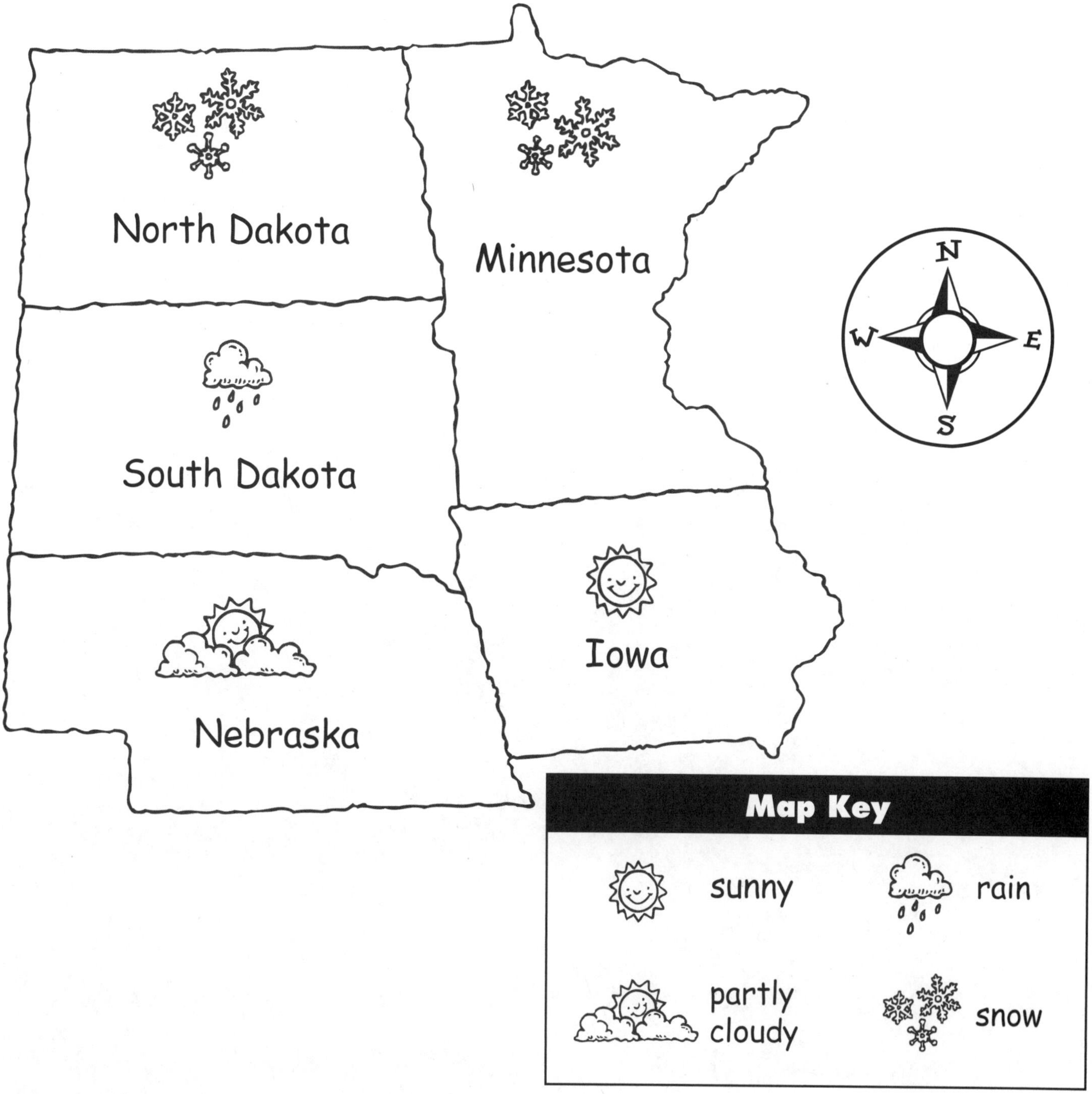

I like the state of ______________________.

The weather is ______________________.

A Desert Habitat

This desert is hot and dry. It has rocky and sandy land. Animals live in the desert. Cactus plants live in the desert. People live in the desert. The desert is their habitat. It is their home.

Moving to the City

The Brown family is moving. Mr. and Mrs. Brown have new jobs. They are leaving Springville. They are moving to Parker.

I would like to live in ______________________________.

The population is ______________________ people.

A County Fair Map

A county fair is an outdoor show. People show their animals. They show things they made. There are games, rides, and food.

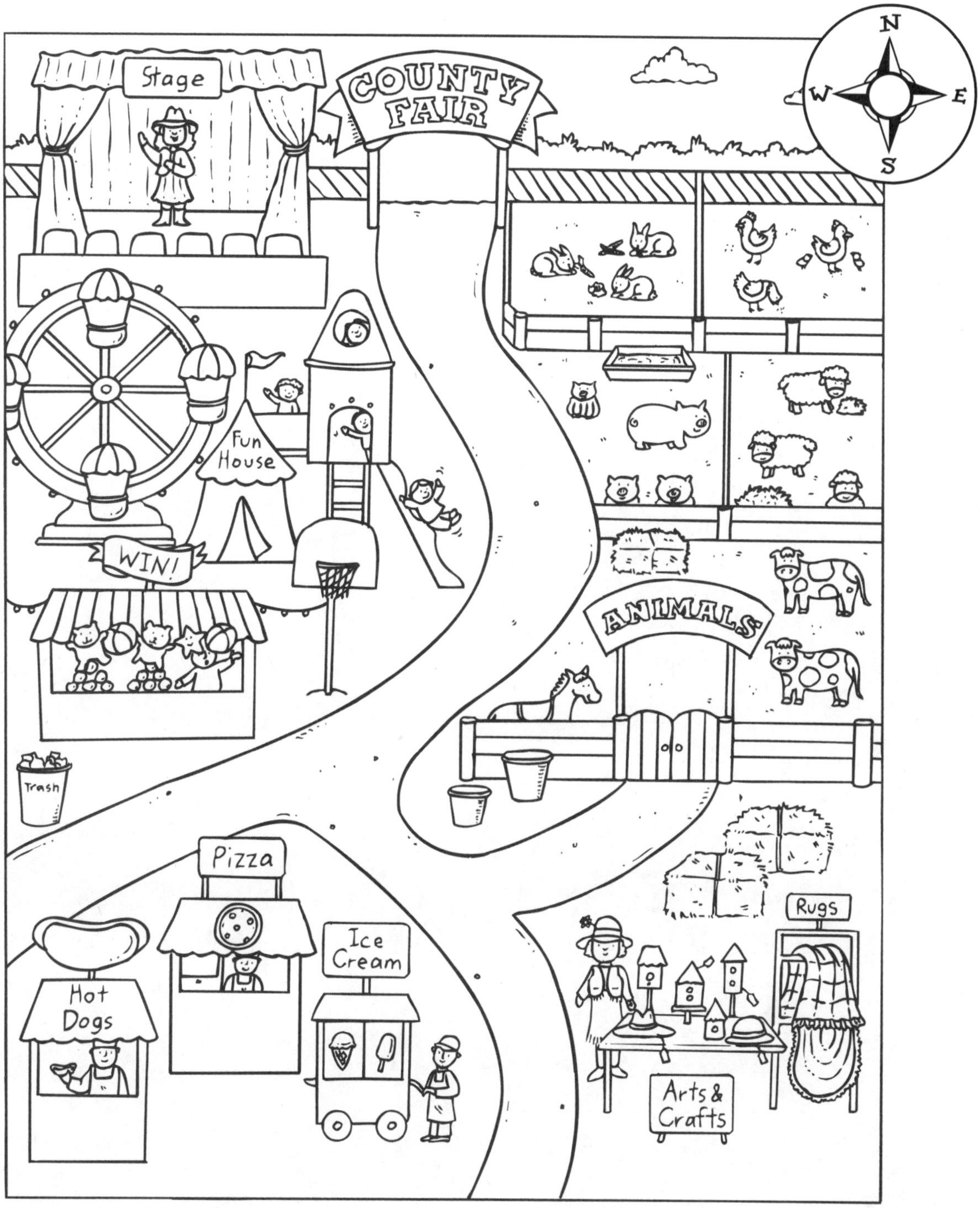

I like the ____________________________ at the county fair.

A Supermarket Map

The supermarket is where you buy products. Products are things that are made and sold.

Homes in a Community

Community Helpers

A community has people who help you. The community helpers work together. They keep you safe and healthy. They help you learn and grow.

Farms in Iowa

There are 87,000 farms in Iowa. Iowa grows the most corn. Iowa grows the most soybeans. Iowa raises the most hogs. Iowa is an important farm state.

Map Key	
Animals Raised	**Plants Grown**
 Beef Cattle	 Corn
 Dairy Cows	 Soybeans
 Hogs	

Visit California!

This is a tourist map of California. It shows fun places to visit.

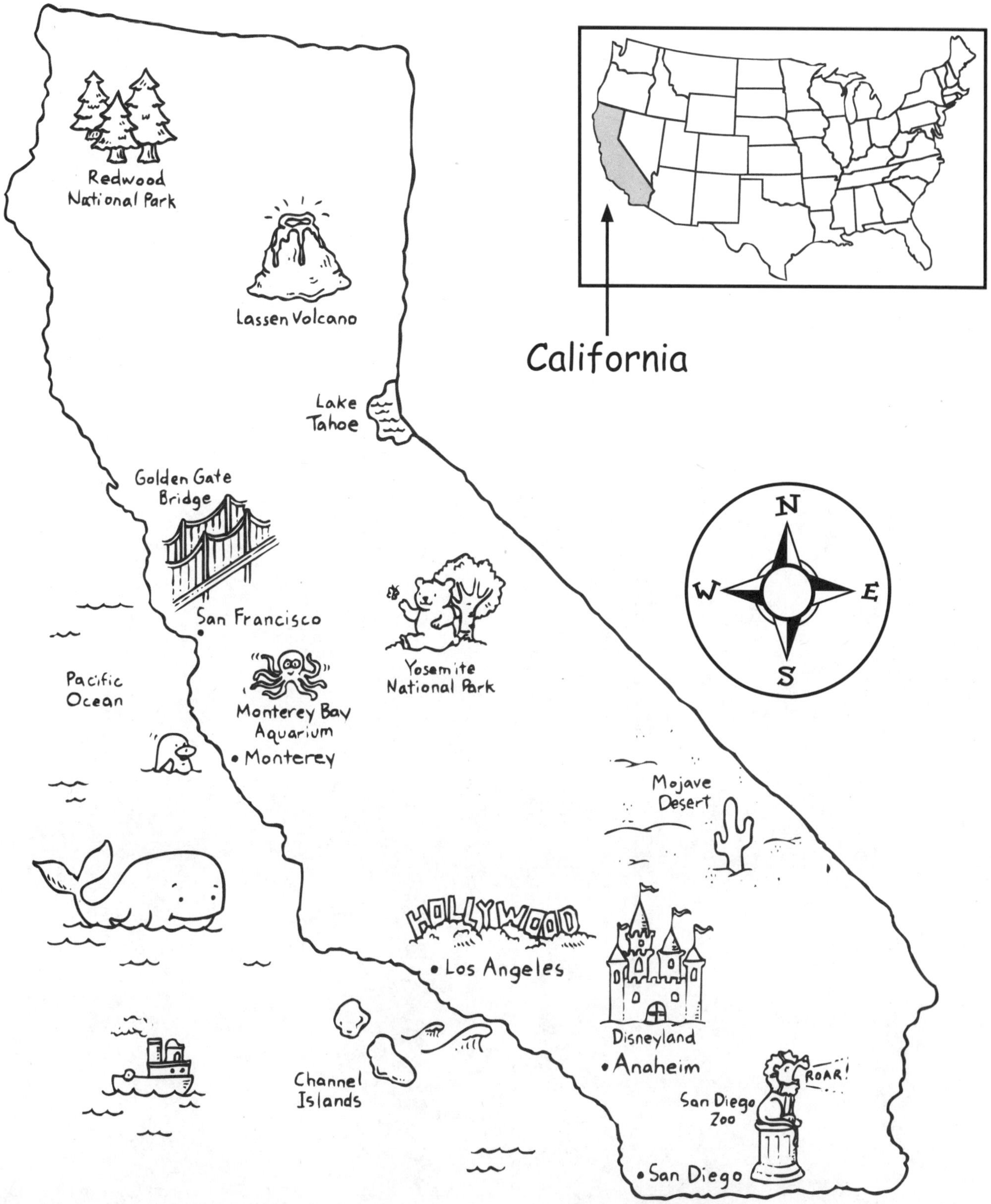

I would like to visit ___________________________________.

Natural Resources of Alaska

Alaska has natural resources. Natural resources are things found in nature. Natural resources are all useful to people.

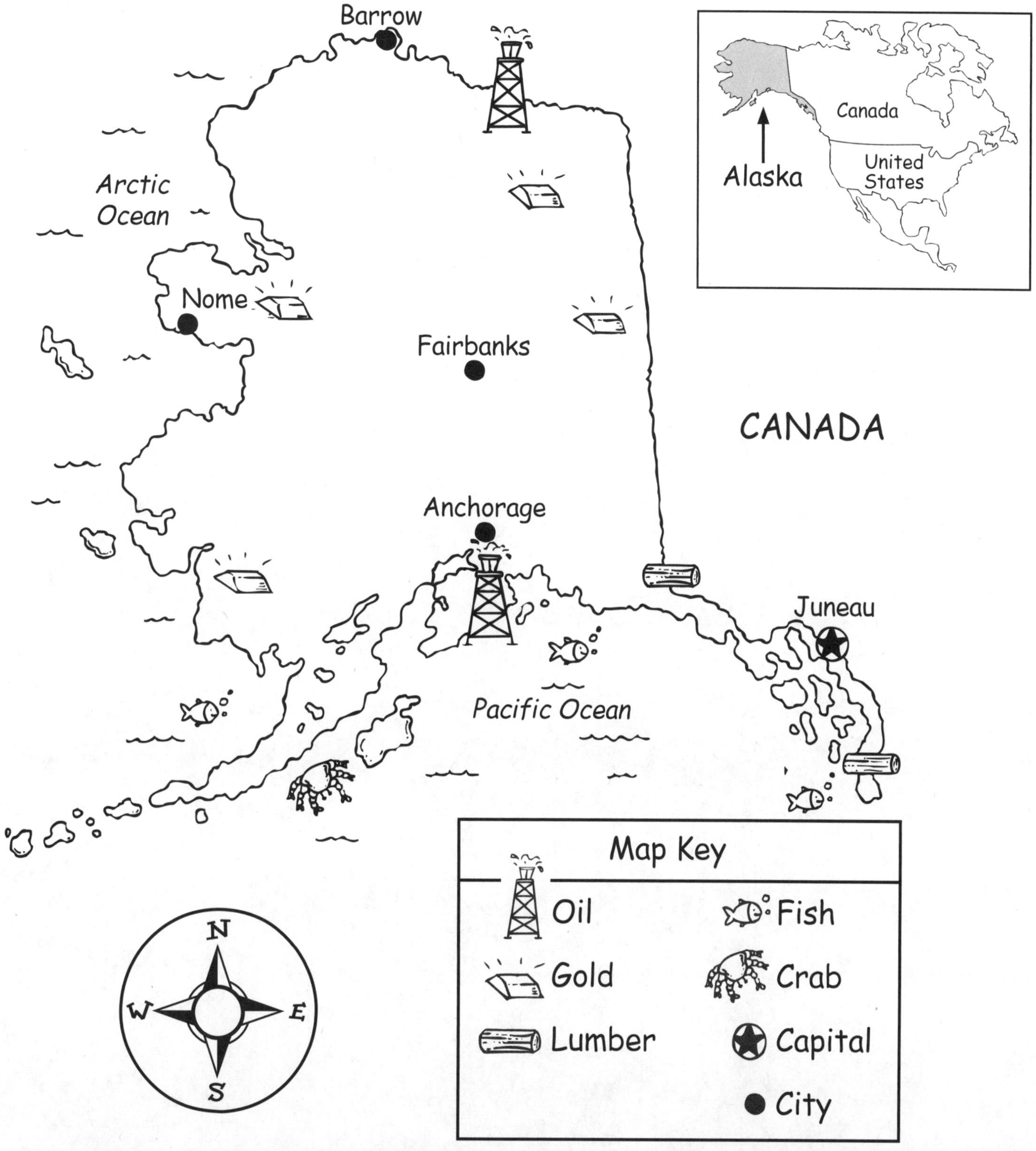

A Frontier Town

This map shows a town from long ago.
What was life like 150 years ago?

A Neighborhood Plan

The map shows a neighborhood. There is an empty lot.

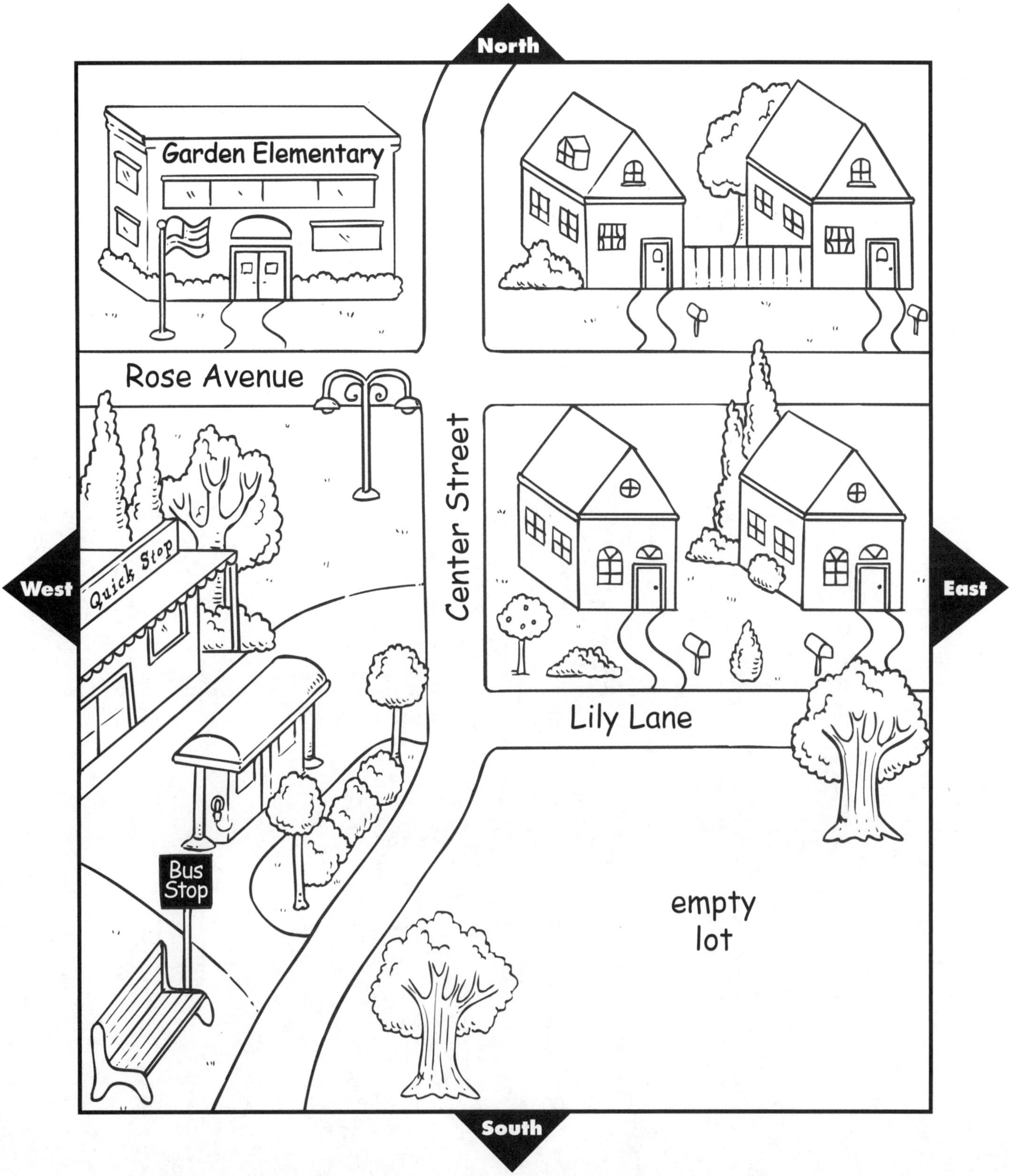